Netv

Paddy Chayefsky, born Sidney Aaron Chayefsky on 29 January 1923, was one of the seminal dramatists of the twentieth century. Emerging as a powerful voice from the 'golden age' of American television, Chayefsky went on to achieve success as a playwright, screenwriter and novelist – winning three Academy Awards, a record for a solo screenwriter. He grew up in The Bronx and graduated from City College of New York in 1943 with a Bachelor of Special Studies and later studied languages at Fordham University. Originally intending to become a comedian, he turned to writing while recovering from injuries sustained from a land mine as a soldier in the Second World War. After the war, he wrote short stories, radio scripts and gags for personalities like Robert Q. Lewis, and episodes for early TV shows like *Danger* and *Manhunt*. In the 1950s, he started to achieve national prominence for his teleplays which were broadcast live on the 'Goodyear-Philco Television Playhouse', among others *Holiday Song* (1952), *Printer's Measure* (1953), *Marty* (1953), *The Bachelor Party* (1953), *The Mother* (1954), *Middle of the Night* (1954), *The Catered Affair* (1955), and *The Great American Hoax* (1956). His films include an adaptation of his teleplay *Marty* (1955, Oscar for Best Screenplay and Best Picture); *The Goddess* (1958, nominated Oscar for Best Screenplay); *Middle of the Night* (1959); *The Americanization of Emily* (1964); *The Hospital* (1971, Oscar for Best Screenplay) *Network* (1976, Oscar for Best Screenplay), and *Altered States* (1980, adapted from his novel). His plays include *Middle of the Night* (1956), *The Tenth Man* (1959, Tony Award nominee Best Play), *Gideon* (1961, Tony Award nominee Best Play), *The Passion of Josef D.* (1964, also director) and *The Latent Heterosexual* (1967). He passed away on 1 August 1981.

Lee Hall was born in Newcastle in 1966. He started writing for radio in 1995, winning awards for *I Luv You Jimmy Spud*, *Spoonface Steinberg* and *Blood Sugar*, all of which made the journey to other media. His screenplay for *Billy Elliot* was nominated for an Oscar and adapted into a multi-award-winning stage musical. *The Pitmen Painters* received the Evening Standard Best Play Award and TMA Best New Play Award. *Our Ladies of Perpetual Succour* won the Olivier Award for Best New Comedy in 2017. He has worked as writer-in-residence for Live Theatre, Newcastle, and the Royal Shakespeare Company. His many adaptations for the stage include Goldoni's *A Servant to Two Masters*, Brecht's *Mr Puntila and His Man Matti* and Heijermans' *The Good Hope*. His adaptation for film of *Victoria & Abdul*, based on the book by Shrabani Basu, was released in 2017.

Network

adapted for the stage by
LEE HALL

based on the film by
PADDY CHAYEFSKY

FABER & FABER

First published in 2017
by Faber and Faber Limited
74–77 Great Russell Street
London WC1B 3DA

Typeset by Country Setting, Kingsdown, Kent CT14 8ES
Printed in England by CPI Group (UK) Ltd, Croydon CR0 4YY

All rights reserved

A CIP record for this book is available from the British Library

ISBN 978-0-571-34546-5

FSC
www.fsc.org
MIX
Paper from
responsible sources
FSC® C020471

2 4 6 8 10 9 7 5 3 1

Introduction

I have long wanted to bring Paddy Chayefsky's drama *Network* to the stage. I remember being thrilled when I first saw the film in the early 1990s in New York. I was baffled why it wasn't as well known in Britain as it is in the States, where it has a cult status. The writing is brilliant and coruscating. The image of a man losing it, and that anger being absorbed and manipulated by the capitalist machine seems an abiding fable. Watching the movie again about ten years ago I realised that Chayefsky's analysis of seventies TV could equally apply to the internet. His understanding that what you see isn't necessarily what you are getting seemed amazingly prescient. So I made my first bid to try to see if the stage rights were available. I was initially thwarted by the complex maze which always entangles anything that was first written as a movie, but was amazed to get a call from producers who did eventually manage to unpick everything. They had no idea of my existing interest but I gratefully grabbed the opportunity.

I was very keen to ensure that Paddy's vision was as unsullied as I could make it. Almost every word in the adaptation is actually Paddy's. I was given access to his notebooks and papers which are housed in the New York Public Library and I pieced together various insights he had about the script retrospectively. If you watch the interviews with him just after the film came out you sense a man who is still struggling to get a handle on the new world order he is drawing on screen. It's like he's almost unwittingly stumbled upon something and is trying to keep up with his own invention. I've tried to include these thoughts and his passionate articulations about what the film is about in an act I like to think of as 'keyhole surgery'. Hopefully my interventions are invisible to the untrained eye.

What I had not bargained for when I took on the adaptation was how prescient it would be about our own Age of Anger. As a fable about how the media and corporate interests can exploit the very discontent they cause, it feels current and chilling. Chayefsky's satire has become almost documentary realism. The only element which seemed stuck in the seventies was the depiction of the terrorists as cynical media whores. Both Ivo and I felt that terrorism's relationship to the media is now very different from those salad days when it might have been acceptable to poke fun at the supposed radical chic of the Black Power movement. I think we all feel terrorism is difficult to laugh at and not something we can so easily laugh off any more. But other than those cheap jibes at Stokely Carmichael this is unadulterated Chayefsky replete with some of the best dramatic writing and brilliant invective of the last fifty years. I think he's one of the great American dramatists and would urge anyone to track down *The Hospital* or *Marty* or indeed any of his other plays or screenplays if you want to see a master at their game.

Thanks to Dan Chayefsky and Patrick Myers for allowing me to work on this, and Rufus Norris and the extraordinary Ivo van Hove for bringing it to the stage with such care, flair and consideration.

Lee Hall, October 2017

Network, produced in association with Patrick Myles, David Luff, Lee Menzies, Ros Povey and Dean Stolber, was first performed on the Lyttelton stage of the National Theatre, London, on 13 November 2017. The cast, in alphabetical order. was as follows:

Harry Hunter Charles Babalola
Technician Tobi Bamtefa
Arthur Jensen Richard Cordery
Howard Beale Bryan Cranston
Secretary Isabel Della-Porta
Diana Christensen Michelle Dockery
Director Ian Drysdale
Edward Ruddy Michael Elwyn
Louise Schumacher Caroline Faber
Jack Snowden Robert Gilbert
Max Schumacher Douglas Henshall
Nelson Chaney Tom Hodgkins
Frank Hackett Tunji Kasim
Technician Andrew Lewis
Technician Beverley Longhurst
Schlesinger Evan Milton
Floor Manager Stuart Nunn
Technician Rebecca Omogbehin
Continuity Announcer Patrick Poletti
ELA Member Danny Szam
Sheila Paksie Vernon

On Film
News Reporters Julie Armstrong,
 Sian Polhill-Thomas and Sid Sagar
Verger Adrian Grove
Priest Ian McLarnon

Blindman Quartet
Matt Wright (*Music Director*)
Tom Challenger (*Assistant Music Director*)
Pete Harden
Kit Downes
Jonas De Roover (*Quartet Manager*)

Director Ivo van Hove
Set and Lighting Designer Jan Versweyveld
Video Designer Tal Yarden
Costume Designer An D'Huys
Music and Sound Eric Sleichim
Fight Director Kevin McCurdy
Company Voice Work Jeannette Nelson
Dialect Coach Charmian Hoare
Staff Director Jaz Woodcock-Stewart

The production was played without an interval

Characters

Howard Beale
anchorman

Harry Hunter
associate producer

Max Schumacher
Head of News

Frank Hackett
executive

Louise
his wife

Ed Ruddy
chairman

Diana Christiensen
Director of Programming

Schlesinger
her researcher

Nelson Chaney
executive

Jack Snowden
presenter

Mr Jensen
Head of UBS

Director

Production Assistant

Floor Manager

Continuity Announcer

Outside Broadcaster

Technician

Assistant Cameraman

Secretaries

Warm-up Guy

ELA Member

NETWORK

Act One

SCENE ONE
PRELUDE TO THE NEWS HOUR

Chaos of voices.
  TV shows.
  Channels of news.
  Ads.
  Soaps.

All talking at once, across several different networks.

A TV studio,
  Cameras roll into position.
  A cacophony of voices from the studio floor,
  Voices from the control booth boom over the PA.

*The Director and Production Assistant are always in the
control booth – but the conversations they are having via
their headsets are amplified for us. The Floor Manager
answers them through his headset which is also amplified
so we can hear.*

Production Assistant One minute to go.

Floor Manager One minute to go.

Director Can we have Howard, please?

Floor Manager Can we have Howard?

Production Assistant Continuity on air in fifty-five
seconds.

Floor Manager Fifty-five seconds and counting.
  Howard. Where the hell is Howard?

Howard is brought on followed by his make-up and costume people. Projected signs tell us the story:

THIS IS THE STORY OF HOWARD BEALE

Howard takes his seat and receives last-minute attention.

THE NETWORK NEWS ANCHOR MAN
FOR UBS-TV

And Harry Hunter, Associate Producer, is running through the order of things privately with Howard, referring to a clipboard.

Harry Hunter Patty Hearst, the Middle East, Rust Belt closures, OPEC . . .

MANDARIN OF TELEVISION

While final checks are made we hear more voices from the control room:

Director Give me A-Camera. Do we have sound?

Floor Manager Check.

Production Assistant Thirty seconds.

Nervous tension, people dashing round executing the last-minute technical stuff. Harry Hunter leaves for the control room.

Director B-Camera.

Floor Manager Check.

Director Sound.

Floor Manager Check.

GRAND OLD MAN OF THE NEWS

Director Howard?

Floor Manager Check.

We are see a plethora of ads for soap powder, tacos, hair products, diarrhoea pills.

LOST A SIX-POINT SHARE IN 1972

The make-up artist and costume person have finished and rush away from Howard's desk.
Howard prepares himself, shuffling through his papers.

Director Studio ready?

COINCIDING WITH HIS WIFE'S DEATH

Floor Manager Studio ready.

In the control room the countdown starts:

Production Assistant Ten . . . nine . . . eight . . .

The ads conclude.

LEAVING HIM A CHILDLESS WIDOWER

Seven . . . six . . . five . . .

Director Continuity.

The Continuity Announcer appears on the monitors telling us:

Continuity Announcer It's time for *Tonight*, with Howard Beale.

Howard takes a swig of water.

WITH AN ALCOHOL PROBLEM

Director Cue music.

Production Assistant Three . . . two . . . one . . .

AN 8 RATING

The theme music blasts out, the Floor Manager is shouting over the top of this.

AND 12 SHARE

Floor Manager Titles, credits, camera, and *Howard*!

Howard (*on camera*) Good evening. It is Friday, September the nineteenth 1975, and I am Howard Beale. Today reaction to the capture of Patty Hearst –

The newscast magically carries on on-screen while Howard moves to the bar, where he joins Max.

– granddaughter of the publisher William Randolph Hearst, in Morse Street, San Francisco. Police reveal images of the moment they apprehended the original kidnappers William and Emily Harris. Hearst, who had eluded capture for nineteen months became part of the so-called Symbionese Liberation Army . . .

AND WAS FIRED BY HIS BEST FRIEND, MAX SCHUMACHER, AFTER THE EVENING NEWS

SCENE TWO
HOWARD AND MAX ARE DRUNK

As the newscast ends we join Howard and Max's conversation:

Howard Twenty-five years, Max. I came over from CBS in '51. Can you believe it? They were just building the lower level on the George Washington Bridge – I remember just after I started they were doing a remote there. Except nobody told me. Then ten after seven in the morning, I get a call. 'Where the hell are you? You're supposed to be on the George Washington Bridge!' I jump

6

out of bed, run downstairs, I get out in the street, I flag a cab, jump in. I say, 'Take me to the middle of the George Washington Bridge!' The driver turns round. He says, 'Don't do it, buddy. You're a young man, you've got your whole life ahead of you.'

They break into uncontrollable laughter.

I think I'm going to kill myself.

Max Oh shit, Howard.

Howard I'm going to blow my brains out right on air, right in the middle of the seven o'clock news.

Max You'll get a hell of a rating, I'll tell you that. A fifty share. Easy.

Howard You think so?

Max Sure. We could make a series out of it. 'Suicide of the Week'. Hell, why limit ourselves? 'Execution of the Week'. Every Sunday night, settle down and watch someone get hung, drawn and quartered. For a logo we'll have some brute with a black hood over his head. Think of the spin-offs.

Howard 'Terrorist of the week'.

Max I love it. Suicides, assassinations, mad bombers, human sacrifices in witches' covens.

Howard 'The Death Hour'. A great Sunday-night show for all the family. Wipe Disney right off the air.

They laugh again.

Max I really am sorry, Howard.

*Chaos of voices, news feeds, ads etc., back exactly where
we were in the opening scene.*

Images of all channels. Cameras are put into position.

*Voices call from the control room – but this time we
also follow the conversation that is going on within the
control room alongside the cacophony of voices on the
news set.*

*The Production Assistant, the Director and Harry
Hunter are all in the control booth, with others.*

Production Assistant One minute to go.

Floor Manager One minute to go.

Director Can we have Howard, please?
OK. We run the Presidential item. How long is
Snowden's package?

Harry Hunter One-twenty.

Director Continuity. Going on air in fifty-three seconds.
One-twenty. Tag on Ron Neeson. Then cut to the ads.
Open the second segment with the the Iranian piece and
the terrorist report. All good.
Can we have Howard, please?

Floor Manager Fifty-five seconds to broadcast.
Howard.

*Howard walks confidently on to the set followed by
make-up and wardrobe.*

Harry Hunter Are we using Squeaky Fromme?

Production Assistant Give me A-camera. Do we have
sound?

Director No, Snowden nixed Squeaky Fromme.

Floor Manager Check.

Harry Hunter But we are keeping the map in?

Director B-Camera.
Yes, keep the map. Hold the news-pix.

Floor Manager Check.

Director Sound.

Floor Manager Check.

A countdown is taking place, nervous tension, people dash round executing the last-second technical stuff.

Production Assistant Howard.

Floor Manager Check.

Director Studio ready?

Floor Manager Studio ready.

We see the ad breaks. The make-up artist and costume person rush away from Howard's desk. In the control room the countdown starts
The ads conclude.

Production Assistant Ten . . . nine . . . eight . . . seven . . . six . . .

Director Continuity.

Production Assistant Five . . . four . . .

Continuity Announcer It's time for *Tonight*, with Howard Beale.

Director Music.

Howard takes a swig of water.

Production Assistant Three . . . two . . . one.

The theme music blasts out, the Floor Manager is shouting over the top of this:

Floor Manager Titles, credits, camera, and *Howard*!

Howard Good evening. It is Monday, September the twenty-second 1975, and I am Howard Beale. Today, a shot was fired at President Ford's motorcade in San Francisco. The President was unharmed. The incident happened late this afternoon just seventeen days after an attempt on his life in Sacramento. The shot was fired as Mr Ford was leaving the St Francis Hotel on his way to the airport. Our reporter Jack Snowden reports from the scene.

As Howard hands over to Snowden, the make-up person comes on to set and administers more make-up. We see Snowden doing his piece to camera on the monitors around the studio and in the auditorium.

Snowden (*on monitor*) The first attempt on President Ford's life was seventeen days ago, and again today in San Francisco. In spite of two attempts, Mr Ford said in a press conference he will not become a prisoner of the Oval Office . . .

All the while a Technical Director does a countdown while Snowden's report is on air.
We also hear the conversation in the control room.

Director Cue Jack.
Sheila, d'ya wanna get a drink later?

Production Assistant I can't, I said I'd see Jeff from downstairs.

Harry Hunter Jeff?! You realise he's a married man.

Production Assistant I happen to like married men.

Harry Hunter Sheila, if you are so hot for married men, why go to strangers? What's wrong with me?

Snowden (*on monitor*) A hostage of would-be assassins . . .

Production Assistant Headroll . . . rolling . . .
  Counting. Twenty seconds . . . nineteen . . .

President Ford (*on monitor*) The American people are good people. Democrats, Independents, Republicans and others. Under no circumstances will I capitulate –

Production Assistant Eighteen . . . seventeen . . . sixteen . . . fifteen . . . fourteen . . . thirteen . . . twelve . . . eleven . . . ten . . .

President Ford – to those who want to undercut all that's good in America.

Director Clear make-up. Prepare sound.

Floor Manager Clear make-up. Prepare sound.

Production Assistant Seven . . . six . . . five . . . four . . . (three, two, one).

Floor Manager And . . . cue Howard.

  Howard is back on air.

Howard Ladies and gentlemen, I would like at this moment to announce that I will be retiring from this programme in two weeks' time because of poor ratings –

Director Pull out to Camera-B.

Howard But since this show was the only thing I had going for me in my life, I have decided to kill myself . . .

Director And cut to Camera-A.

Howard I'm going to blow my brains out right on this programme a week from today.

Production Assistant Ten seconds to commercial. Nine . . . eight . . . seven . . . (*Etc.*)

Howard So tune in next Tuesday. That'll give the public relations people a week to promote the show. That ought to get a hell of a rating, a 50 share at least. I'll be back after these messages from our sponsors.

Production Assistant Three . . . two . . . one.

Director And commercial break. Cue VT-A. (*To Howard through the public address system.*) Thank you, Howard.
C'mon, just one drink won't harm you.

Floor Manager Jesus Christ. Did you hear what he said?

The ad for cat food is playing. Howard calmly takes a glass of water.

Director What?

Floor Manager Howard just said he was going to blow his brains out.

Director What are you talking about?

Floor Manager Didn't you hear him?

Harry Hunter Are you serious?

Floor Manager Howard just said he was going to kill himself on the show next Tuesday.

Director What do you mean, he said he was going to kill himself next Tuesday?

Harry Hunter He was supposed to do a tag on Ron Neeson and go to commercial.

Director (*to Howard, through the address system*) Did you say you were going to kill yourself on air?

Howard Yes.

Production Assistant We are on air in thirty seconds.

Harry Hunter (*through the address system*) What the fuck is going on, Howard?

Howard fiddles with his ear piece.

Howard I can't hear you?

Floor Manager They want to know what the fuck is going on, Howard.

Howard Can I have more water?

Harry Hunter runs into the studio from the control booth.

Harry Hunter Jesus Christ, Howard. Is this some kind of joke?

Howard No. I am going to kill myself on air next Tuesday.

Production Assistant Twenty seconds . . .

Harry Hunter What the hell's going on, Howard, have you completely lost the plot?

Floor Manager What d'ya want me to do?

Director We've still got to do the Ron Neeson tag and the piece on Iran. (*Through the address system.*) What the fuck's going on down there?

Howard I don't see what all the fuss is about.

Harry Hunter I think we have to get him off.
Howard, I'm afraid we'll have to take you off.

Howard I am not going anywhere.

Harry Hunter Howard, I am asking you to step down from the chair.

Howard Absolutely not. I am reading the news.

Production Assistant Ten seconds and counting . . .

She counts down over:

Floor Manager What the hell are we gonna do?

Director Ready, Camera-A . . . ready, sound.

Harry Hunter What the fuck are you doing, Howard? Get off that seat.

Director What the hell is going on down there? We're back to the studio in six seconds.

Harry Hunter I am the Associate Producer of this programme and I order you to stand down.

The crew start scrabble back to their places. Harry and the Floor Manager hesitate.

Floor Manager What should I do?

Harry Hunter Get him off.

The Floor Manager tries to drag Howard away. Howard clings to the desk. Harry Hunter runs on to help.

Come on, Howard. Let go of the fucking desk.

Production Assistant Three . . . two . . . one . . .

Director Camera-A . . . action.

Howard tries to speak but is being assaulted by Harry Hunter and the Floor Manager.

Howard Welcome back to the Nightly News with / Howard Beale –

Floor Manager For chrissakes, will somebody help us here. He won't let go of the fucking desk.

Other crew members join in the struggle to wrest Howard away.

Harry Hunter Turn off the sound, you stupid son of a bitch. We're going out live!

As the gang of crew members try to pull Howard away from the desk, the Director can be heard from the control booth shouting:

Director What the fuck is going on down there?

Howard Get your hands off me, you bastards.

Howard punches the Floor Manager. Harry Hunter's image is everywhere, screaming:

Harry Hunter Chrissakes! Black it out! This is going out live to sixty-seven affiliates!

Suddenly the live images cut from the screens. A sign appears:

THERE IS A TEMPORARY TECHNICAL PROBLEM
DO NOT ADJUST YOUR SET

SCENE FOUR
THE AFTERMATH

Then the barrage of news stations running the footage, a cacophony of presenters on all the other news channels telling us: 'Tonight UBS anchorman, Howard Beale shocked viewers by announcing his intention to shoot himself on air.' 'Stunned viewers tuned into UBS's nightly news show to hear Howard Beale announce . . .' etc., etc.

Then:

Howard dejected. Frank Hackett in black tie. Max, the Director, Harry Hunter, etc., all shell-shocked.

Hackett You're off the air as of now. First rule of news. You do not become the news.

I'm at supper with the whole of CCA and I'm dragged away for this freak show. And clear out the fucking lobby, every goddam TV station in the city's down there. It's the leading item on every network in the country.

Production Assistant We've had nine hundred calls complaining about the language.

Hackett So what the fuck are we doing to do about it?

Max We're flying Snowden up from Washington. Holloway's gonna read out something at the end of the late show to the effect that Howard's been under great personal stress, etc.

Hackett All right. We've got a stockholders' meeting tomorrow at which we're going to announce the restructuring of the management plan and I don't want this grotesque incident to interfere with any of it. I'll suggest Mr Ruddy open with a short statement washing this whole thing off and you, Max, better have some answers in case some of those nuts that always come to stockholders' meetings start to . . .

Max Mr Beale has been under great personal and professional pressures.

Hackett I've got some goddam surprises for you too, Schumacher. I've had it up to here with your cruddy division and its annual 33-million-dollar deficit.

Max Keep your hands off my news division. We're responsible to corporate level, not you, Hackett.

Hackett We'll goddam well see about that!

Chaney All right, take it easy. Right now, how do we get Beale out of here? I understand there's at least a hundred reporters in the lobby.

Max We'll get a limo at the freight entrance. Howard, you're not gonna talk to anybody till this whole thing calms down, understand?

Hackett And I'll see you at the stockholders' meeting tomorrow afternoon, Schumacher.

SCENE FIVE
THE SCREENING ROOM

Darkness. A film is projected. Grainy footage of a terrorist talking.

Terrorist We live in a society which has never been more technologically able to meet the needs of its people – yet year by year the technology, far from enobling its users, is increasingly an instrument of political quiescence and social control. What is the effect of this 'emancipatory' technology? The rich are becoming exponentially richer whilst the majority are impoverished. Economic segregation runs along racial lines, the ecology of the entire planet is imperilled by the rapacity of the increasingly powerful few, the denuding of everyday life has led to the personal desperation of millions of Americans, we have been lied to by generations of politicians, basic civil liberties are at threat as society becomes increasingly repressive to fuel a capitalist model which not only does not work but is bankrupting our entire economy.

Interviewer's Voice But do you think it's ethical to wage an armed struggle against it?

Terrorist Someone's gonna have to.

The film runs out.

Max Why the hell are you bringing me this? You are Programming. This is News, not Entertainment and Features.

Diana Just wait . . .

The image flickers – now we see something handheld. Footage of people getting out of a car and running across a sidewalk.

Max And what are we looking at now?

Diana You'll see.

We see that the people with the camera person are carrying guns.

Max Jesus Christ, what is this?

They run into a building, start shooting.

Oh my God.

There is chaos. It is verité footage of a terrorist attack, something like the Bataclan incident.

Diana It's the massacre in Detroit.

It is truly horrifying. The tape runs out and Diana is standing in the light of the projector.

Max Where did you get this?

Diana The Ecumenical Liberation Army itself. Admit it. It's pretty sensational.

Max What are you suggesting?

Diana I thought you could use it – make a running feature. Don't you see? We have potential access to actual footage of terrorist actions: hijackings, assassinations, massacres. Each week's segment opens with authentic footage, follow it up with human interest stories of the aftermath.

Max Are you crazy? I can't do that.

Diana Why not?

Max It's completely immoral.

Diana We're not in the business of morality, Mr Schumacher. We are in the business of business. Your antiquated news division is in freefall, Max. Don't you see, the American people want someone to articulate their rage for them. This network hasn't one show in the top twenty. We're an industry joke. I thought I was doing you a favour. If you don't want it I'll have it in Features.

Howard has come in. They both look at him.

Howard Max.

Max What the hell you doing here. I told you to stay at home.

Howard Listen, Max, I'd like another shot.

Max Oh come on, Howard.

Howard I don't mean the whole show. I'd like to come on, make some kind of brief statement, then turn the show over to Jack Snowden. I have twenty-five years at this network, Max. I have some standing in the industry. I don't want to go out like a clown. It'll be simple and dignified. You and Harry can check the copy.
What do you think?

Diana It could take the strain off the show.

Max I'll never get it past Hackett.

Howard Ask him, Max.

SCENE SIX
THE STOCKHOLDERS' CONFERENCE

A huge image of Hackett on screen. A spotlight on him as he addresses the shareholders' meeting on camera. Max is sitting with Chaney, Ruddy and other executives listening the address.

Hackett But the business of management is management. And at the same time CCA took control, the UBS-TV network was foundering with less than seven per cent of national television revenues, most network programmes being sold at station rates. I am therefore pleased to announce I am submitting to the Board of Directors a plan for the coordination of the main profit centres and with the specific intention of developing divisional responsivity to management. Point one. The division producing the lowest return is the News Division with its 98-million-dollar budget and its annual average deficit of 32 million. I know historically news divisions are expected to lose money but to our minds this philosophy is a wanton fiscal affront, to be resolutely resisted. The new plan calls for local news to be transferred to Owned Stations Divisions. News Radio would be transferred to UBS Radio Division, and in effect the News Division would be reduced from an independent division to a streamlined, cost-efficient department accountable to the network.

Hackett steps down from the podium. As the audience applauds:

Max What the hell is this about?

Ruddy Really, this is not the time, Max.

Max Why wasn't I told about this? Why was I led on to this podium and publicly humiliated? Goddammit, I spoke to John Wheeler this morning and he assured me the News Division was safe. Are you trying to get me to resign?

Ruddy We'll talk about this at our regular meeting in the morning. Stick out of the corporate politics, Max. Concentrate on the news.

SCENE SEVEN
BACK IN THE STUDIO

The usual preparations are being made for the start of the news programme.

Production Assistant Two minutes to broadcast.

Director Camera-A.

Floor Manager Check.

Director Camera-B.

Floor Manager Check.

Director Sound.

Floor Manager Check.

Director Can you fix that thing on the front of the desk for me?

Snowden is at the desk being made up.

Jack, are you ready?

Floor Manager (*to make-up and wardrobe*) OK, guys, clear it.

Max marches in with Howard in tow.

Max You need to mike up, Howard. Jack, I'm putting him on. One last time.

Director What is going on down there?

Floor Manager Are you serious?

Max I am putting Howard on air.

Harry Hunter comes rushing in.

Harry Hunter Has Hackett sanctioned this?

Max This is my show, Harry. Howard is going on.

Harry Hunter You can't do this. This is completely irresponsible.

Max I take full responsibility. Howard deserves a chance to go out with some dignity. (*To Snowden.*) I'm sorry, Jack.

Snowden I understand.

Snowden steps down. Howard is miked up and prepared for broadcast.

Harry Hunter I absolutely forbid you to do this. We had a categorical edict from Mr Hackett.

Max Screw you, Hunter. Pull the show if you want to. I am putting Howard on.

Production Assistant Thirty seconds to broadcast.

Harry Hunter Someone call Hackett.

Floor Manager Thirty seconds, clear the stage. Howard is going on. Checks.

Director Sound.

Floor Manager Check.

Director Camera-A.

Floor Manager Check.

Director Camera-B.

Floor Manager Check.

Max You OK, Howard?

Howard Thank you, Max.

Max withdraws. Howard sits, receives some last-minute attention from make-up as the ads are on the bank of screens.

Production Assistant Fifteen seconds.

Max appears in the control room to watch the show

Director Pictures too thick on Camera-B.

Floor Manager Camera-B.

Production Assistant Ten . . . nine . . . eight . . . seven . . . six . . .

Director Continuity.

Continuity Announcer (*on monitor*) It's time for *Tonight* with . . . J— Howard Beale.

Director Cue music.

Production Assistant Five . . . four . . . three . . .

Director Titles, credits, camera, and *Howard*!

Howard Good evening. It is Wednesday. September the twenty-fourth and I am Howard Beale, and this is my last broadcast. Regular viewers will know I announced on this programme that I would commit public suicide, admittedly an act of madness. Well, I wanted to respectfully explain what happened. I just ran out of bullshit . . .

Harry Hunter Jesus Christ. Cut him off.

Max Leave him on.

Harry Hunter Take him off. That's an order.

Max If this is how he wants to go out – this is how he goes out.

Howard Am I still on air?

Max Yes. Say what you have to say, Howard.

Howard (*to camera*) I don't know any other way to say it except I just ran out of bullshit.

Harry Hunter You are finished, Schumacher.

Howard Bullshit is all the reasons we give for living and if we can't think up any reasons of our own, we always have the God bullshit.

Harry Hunter Holy Mary, Mother of Christ. Not that demographic as well.

Howard We don't know why we're going through all this pointless pain, humiliation and decay, so there better be someone somewhere who does know. That's the God bullshit.

Hackett comes into the studio.

Hackett What the hell's going on?

Max He's saying that life is bullshit and it is. What are you screaming about?

Howard If you don't like the God bullshit, how about the man bullshit? Man is a noble creature who can order his own world, so who needs God?

Hackett grabs the Floor Manager's headset to talk to the control room.

Hackett I told you to take the motherfucker off the air.

Max You did.

Hackett Well, get him off the air.

Max Go fuck yourself, Hackett. If you want him off, you go on there and take him off.

Howard Well, if there's anyone out there who can look around this demented slaughterhouse of a world we live in and tell me man is a noble creature, believe me, that man is full of bullshit.

Hackett This is going out to sixty-seven affiliates.

Technicians in the studio laugh.

What's so goddam funny?!

Howard I don't have any kids . . .
  I don't have any kids and I was married for thirty-three years of shrill, shrieking fraud and I don't have any bullshit left.

Production Assistant Ten seconds and counting . . .

Hackett Has he gone completely nuts?

Assistant Cameraman It's the sanest thing I've heard on this network.

Production Assistant Seven . . . six . . . (*Etc.*)

Howard I just ran out of it, you see. That is the news. It has been an honour and privilege to serve you. This is Howard Beale signing off forever.

Director And ad break.

SCENE EIGHT
MAX GETS A DRESSING-DOWN

Max is in Howard's chair. Ruddy is berating him. Nelson Chaney is there watching.

Ruddy The way I hear it, you're the one responsible for this colossally stupid prank. Is that the fact, Max?

Max That's the fact.

Ruddy It was unconscionable. There doesn't seem anything more to say.

Max I have something to say, Ed. I'd like to know why that whole debasement of the News Division announced at the stockholders' meeting this afternoon was kept secret from me. You and I go back twenty years, Ed. I took this job with your personal assurance that you would back my autonomy against any encroachment. But ever since CCA acquired control of the UBS systems ten months ago, Hackett's been taking over everything. Who the hell's running this network, you or some conglomerate called CCA? I mean, you're the President of the Systems group, Hackett's just CCA's hatchet man. Nelson here – for Pete's sake, he's president of the network – he hasn't got a damn thing to say about anything any more.

Ruddy I told you at the stockholders' meeting, Max, that we would discuss all that at our regular meeting tomorrow morning. If you had been patient, I would've explained to you that I too thought Frank Hackett precipitate and that the reorganisation of the News Division would not be executed until everyone, specifically you, Max, had been consulted and satisfied. Instead you sulked off like a child and engaged this network in a shocking and disgraceful episode. Your position here is no longer tenable, regardless of how management is restructured. I will expect your resignation at ten o'clock tomorrow morning and we will coordinate our statement to the least detriment of everyone. Hunter will take over the News Division till we sort this all out.

SCENE NINE
DIANA READS THE NEWS

Diana is at her desk reading the papers as her researcher, Schlesinger, talks to her.

Schlesinger There are four outlines submitted by Universal for an hour series. The first is set in a large eastern law school, presumably Harvard, and is irresistibly called *The New Lawyers*. The running characters are a crusty but benign ex-Supreme Court Justice, a beautiful girl graduate student and a local district attorney who is brilliant but sometimes cuts corners.

Diana Next.

Schlesinger The second is called *The Amazon Squad*. The characters are a crusty but benign police lieutenant who is always getting heat from the commissioner, a hard-nosed, hard-drinking detective who thinks women belong in the kitchen and a beautiful girl cop who –

Diana The Arabs have decided to jack up the price of oil another ten per cent, the CIA have been accused of opening Senator Humphrey's mail, there are three separate wars in the Middle East, New York City is facing default and the whole front page of the *Daily News* is Howard Beale. There is also a two-column story on page one of the *Times*, the *LA Times* and the *Washington Post*. Get me Mr Hackett's office.

SCENE TEN
DIANA MAKES A PITCH

Hackett in his office.

Diana Last night Howard Beale went on the air and yelled bullshit for two minutes and we've got press coverage you couldn't buy for a million dollars. Did you see the overnights on the Network News? It has an eight in New York and a nine in LA and 27 share on both cities. I can tell you right now if we put Beale back on tonight the show will get a 30 share at least. I think we've totally lucked into something.

Hackett Oh for God's sake, are you suggesting we put that lunatic back on the air yelling bullshit?

Diana Yes, I think we should put Beale back on the air tonight and keep him on. Frank, that dumb show jumped five rating points in one night! We just increased our audience by twenty or thirty million people in one night. You're not going to get something like this dumped in your lap for the rest of your days and you just can't piss it away. Howard Beale got up there last night and said what every American feels – that he's tired of all the bullshit. He's articulating the popular rage. I want that show, Frank. I can turn that show into the biggest smash on television.

Hackett What do you mean, you want that show? It's a news show. It's not your department.

Diana I see Howard Beale as a latter-day prophet, a magnificent messianic figure, inveighing against the hypocrites of our times, a nightly Savonarola, Monday through Friday. I tell you, Frank, that could just go through the roof. And I'm talking about a six-dollar cost per thousand show! Do you want to figure out the revenues of a strip show that sells for a hundred thousand bucks a minute? One show like that could pull this whole network right out of the hole. Now, Frank, it's being handed to us on a plate. Let's not blow it.

Intercom buzzes.

Secretary (*on intercom*) John Carlton to see you.

Hackett (*to intercom*) Tell him I'll be a few minutes. Let me think it over.

Diana Frank, let's not go to committee on this. It's twenty after ten and we want Beale in that studio by half past six. We don't want to lose the momentum.

Hackett For God's sake, Diana, we're talking about putting a manifestly irresponsible man on national television.

Diana Yes.

Hackett I'd like to talk to legal affairs at least. You know I'm going to be eyeball-to-eyeball with Mr Ruddy on this. If I'm going to the mat with Ruddy I want to be sure of some of my ground. I am the one whose ass is going on the line.

Diana A hundred thousand a minute, Frank. Fuck Ruddy.

Hackett Let me talk to Chaney. We'll give it a go.

SCENE ELEVEN
A WORKING LUNCH

Chaney and Hackett at a working lunch in the boardroom.

Chaney I don't believe this. I don't believe the top brass of a national television network are sitting round their Caesar salads . . .

Hackett The top brass of a *bankrupt* national television network – with projected losses of close to a 150 million dollars this year.

Chaney I don't care how bankrupt! You can't seriously be proposing – and the rest of us seriously considering – putting on a pornographic network news show! The FCC will kill us.

Hackett The FCC can't do anything except rap our knuckles.

Chaney I don't even want to think about the litigious possibilities, Frank. Anyway, no affiliates are gonna carry it.

Hackett The affiliates will kiss your fat ass if you can hand them a hit show.

Chaney The popular reaction –

Hackett We don't know the popular reaction. That's what we have to find out.

Chaney The *Times* –

Hackett The *New York Times* doesn't advertise on our network.

Chaney All I know is that this violates every canon of respectable broadcasting.

Hackett We're not a respectable network. We're a whorehouse network and we have to take whatever we can get.

Chaney Well, I don't want any part of it. I don't fancy myself the president of a whorehouse.

Hackett That's very commendable of you, Nelson. Now, sit down. Your indignation has been duly recorded, you can always resign tomorrow. Look, what in substance are we proposing? Merely to add editorial comment to our network news show. Brinkley, Sevareid and Reasoner all have their comments. So now Howard Beale will have his. I think we ought to give it a shot. Let's see what happens tonight. Telephone.

Chaney I may be in charge here but I don't want to be the Babylonian messenger who has to tell Max Schumacher about this.

Hackett Max Schumacher no longer works at this network. Mr Ruddy fired him last night. Harry Hunter is running the News Division now. Phone.

Chaney passes Hackett the phone.

Hunter in News, please.

SCENE TWELVE
MAX AND HOWARD PACK UP

Howard Fifty-two years between us in two cardboard boxes. What are we going to do?

Max Teach? Write a book? Whatever the hell one does in the autumn of one's years. It had to come sooner or later.

Howard What's that?

Max It's us at NBC with Ed Murrow and the gang.

Howard takes the picture.

Howard My God, is that me? Were we ever that young? Is that Cronkite? He looked old even then. Who is that?

Max Remember that kid who we sent out to interview Cleveland Amory on vivisection?

Howard Oh yes! Yes.

They laugh.
A Secretary walks in.

Secretary Everybody's waiting.

SCENE THIRTEEN
HOWARD GIVES HIS FAREWELL SPEECH

Howard is surrounded by people enjoying his speech.

Howard . . . So I jump out of bed, run down stairs . . . I get out in the street, I flag a cab, jump in. I say. 'Take me to the middle of the George Washington Bridge!' The driver turns round. He says, 'Don't do it, buddy. You're a young man, you've got your whole life ahead of you.'

General hilarity. Harry Hunter comes in.

Harry Hunter Well, if you think that's funny, wait till you hear this. I've just had a call from Hackett and he wants to put Howard back on the air tonight. Apparently the ratings jumped five points last night. And he wants Howard to go back on and do his angry man thing.

Howard What are you talking about?

Harry Hunter I'm telling you. They want Howard to go back on and yell bullshit. They want Howard to go on spontaneously venting his anger, a latter-day prophet, denouncing the hypocrisies of our times.

Howard Sounds pretty good.

Max Who is this 'they'?

Harry Hunter Hackett and Chaney had a meeting, they've passed it by legal affairs, apparently that girl from Programming was there.

Max What's she got to do with it?

Howard You're kidding, right?

Harry Hunter I'm not kidding. I told them, 'Forget it. We're running a news department down there, not a circus. And Howard Beale isn't a bearded lady. And if you think I'll go along with this bastardisation of the news you can have my resignation along with Max Schumacher's right now. And I think I'm speaking for Howard Beale and everyone else down there in News.'

Howard Hold on. What's wrong with being an angry prophet denouncing the hypocrisies of our times? What do you think, Max?

Max Do you want to be an angry prophet denouncing the hypocrisies of our times?

He thinks.

Howard Yeah, I think I'd like to be an angry prophet denouncing the hypocrisies of our times.

Max Then grab it.

The company cheer.

SCENE FOURTEEN
MAX CHALLENGES RUDDY

Max alone. Ruddy enters.

Ruddy Chaney tells me Beale may actually go on the air this evening.

Max As far as I know, Howard's gonna do it. Are you actually gonna sit still for this, Ed?

Ruddy Yes, I think Hackett's overstepped himself. This isn't about Howard, this is corporate manoeuvring. Hackett is clearly forcing a confrontation. That would account for his behaviour at the stockholders' meeting. However, I think he's making a serious mistake with this Beale business. I suspect CCA will be upset by Hackett's presumptuousness and certainly Mr Jensen will. So I'm going to let Hackett have his head for a while. He just might lose it over this Beale business. I'd like you to reconsider your resignation. I have to assume whatever Hackett does, he's gonna take the CCA Board so I'll have to appeal directly to Mr Jensen. When that happens I'm gonna need every friend I've got. And I certainly don't want Hackett's people in all the divisional positions. So I'm putting you back in charge, Max.

33

Max To preside over Howard making a complete fool of himself and everybody else.

Ruddy I'm afraid so.

Max OK.

Ruddy Thank you, Max.

SCENE FIFTEEN
HOWARD BACK ON AIR

Back in the studio the machine grinds on as usual:

Production Assistant One minute to go.

Floor Manager One minute to go.

Director Can we have Howard, please?

Floor Manager Can we have Howard?

Production Assistant Continuity on air in fifty-five seconds.

Floor Manager Fifty-five seconds and counting. Howard. Where the hell is Howard?

Howard is brought on, followed by his make-up and costume people.

Director Give me Camera-A. Do we have sound?

Floor Manager Check.

Production Assistant Thirty seconds.

Director Camera-B.

Floor Manager Check.

Director Sound.

Floor Manager Check.

Director Howard.

Floor Manager Check.

Director Studio ready?

Floor Manager Studio ready.

Production Assistant Ten . . . nine . . . eight . . . seven . . . six. . . . five . . .

Director Continuity.

Continuity Announcer It's time for *Tonight*, with Howard Beale.

Director Cue music.

Production Assistant Three . . . two . . . one.

Director Titles, credits, camera, and *Howard*!

Howard Good evening. It is Thursday, September the twenty-fifth and I am Howard Beale, still bringing you the news. Today at a meeting of OPEC the Arabs have decided to jack up the price of oil another twenty per cent – has anybody done anything about it? Nope. President Ford has convened another meeting of the IFA to do, surprise surprise, nothing in particular. If that's not bad enough, unemployment figures are up another five per cent, there are more closures in the Rust Belt, and the CIA has finally admitted opening Senator Humphrey's mail, but we all know we can trust the CIA, can't we? Basically, business as usual. And let's not forget: there's a civil war in Angola –

Howard's speech is broadcast on a TV in Max's office.

Max is watching Howard on TV.

Howard (*on TV*) – another one in Beirut. New York City is facing default. And there are terrorists on the loose out there. One damned thing after another. Day after day after day. And what I'm asking is: when is this going to stop?

> *Max turns off the TV. In the studio, we see the end of the broadcast, Howard taking off his mike, the studio closing down. But we are focused on Max's room. Diana has entered, and surprises Max.*

Diana The Thursday show rated 14 with a 37 share, the Friday show rated 11 with a 30 share, and Monday's show is down another three points. It's gonna to need some help if it's going to hold, Max. Beale doesn't do the angry man thing well at all. He's too kvetchy. He's being irascible. We want a prophet, not a curmudgeon. He should do more 'Day of Wrath', apocalyptic doom. I think you should take on a couple of writers to write some jeremiads for him. I see you don't like my suggestions.

Max Hell, you're not being serious, are you?

Diana Oh, I am being totally serious. The fact is, I could make your Beale show the highest rated news show in television if you'd let me have a crack at it.

Max What do you mean, 'have a crack at it'?

Diana I'd like to programme it for you, develop it. I wouldn't interfere with the actual news. But teevee is showbiz, Max, and even the news has to have a little showmanship. What we need is someone who cuts through this anodyne crap we peddle as news. We need someone who reminds us who we are.

Max My God, you are serious.

Diana I watched your six o'clock show today, it's straight tabloid. You had a minute and a half on that lady riding a bike naked in Central Park. On the other hand you had less than a minute of hard national and international news. It was all sex, scandal, brutal crimes, sports, children with incurable diseases and lost puppies. So I don't think I'll listen to any protestations of high standards of journalism. You're right down in the street soliciting audiences like the rest of us. All I'm saying is, if you're going to hustle at least do it right. I'm going to bring this up at tomorrow's network meeting, but I don't like network hassles, and I was hoping you and I could work this out between us. That's why I'm here right now.

Max And I was hoping you were looking for an emotional involvement with a craggy middle-aged man.

Diana I wouldn't rule that out entirely.

Max Well, Diana, you bring all your ideas up at the meeting tomorrow, because if you don't I will. I think Howard is making a goddam fool of himself and so does everybody Howard and I know in this industry. It was a fluke. It didn't work. Tomorrow, Howard goes back to the old format and this gutter depravity comes to an end.

Diana OK.

Max I don't get it, Diana. You hung around till half past seven and came all the way down here just to pitch this crazy idea when you knew goddam well I'd laugh you out of this office. I don't get it. What's your scam in this?

Diana Max, my little visit here tonight was just a courtesy made out of respect for your stature in the industry and because I've personally admired you ever since I was a kid majoring in Speech at the University of Missouri. But sooner or later, with or without you, I'm going to take over your network news show and I figured I might as well start tonight.

Max I think I once gave a lecture at the University of Missouri.

Diana I was in the audience. I had a terrible schoolgirl crush on you for a couple of months.

Max If we can get back for a moment to the bit of the conversation where you hadn't ruled out emotional involvements with middle-aged men . . . What are you doing for dinner tonight?

Diana calls somebody.

Diana I can't make it tonight, love. Call me tomorrow.

Max Do you have any favourite restaurants?

Diana I eat anything.

Max Son of a bitch, I get the feeling I'm being made.

Diana You are.

Max I better warn you, I don't do anything on the first date.

Diana We'll see about that.

SCENE SEVENTEEN
HOWARD HAS A VISION

Suddenly Howard appears out of the darkness like a ghost. His face is lit up – he is clearly terrified.

Howard Hello. Hello?

He listens intently.

I can't hear you. Speak a little louder.
   Yes. Yes. Yes.

He appears to hear something we cannot.

Why me? I said, why me?

He listens again, then answers.

OK!
OK!

SCENE EIGHTEEN
THE HIP RESTAURANT

Diana and Max have supper.

Diana I was married for four years and pretended to
be happy and had six years of analysis and pretended
to be sane. My husband ran off with his boyfriend and
I had an affair with my analyst. He told me I was the
worst lay he had ever had. I can't tell you how many men
have told me what a lousy lay I am. I apparently have a
masculine temperament. I arouse quickly, consummate
prematurely and can't wait to get my clothes back on and
get out of the bedroom. I seem to be inept at everything
except my work. I'm good at my work and so I confine
myself to that. All I want out of life is a 30 share and a
20 rating. You're married surely?

Max Twenty-five years. I have a married daughter in
Seattle who's six months pregnant and a younger girl
who starts Northwestern in January.

Diana Well, Max, here we are. Middle-aged man
reaffirming his middle-aged manhood and a terrified
young woman with a father complex. What sort of script
do you think we can make out of this?

Max Terrified?

Diana Out of my skull. I'm the hip generation, man,

right on, cool, groovy, the greening of America, remember all that? God, what humbugs we were. In my first year at college I lived in a commune, dropped acid daily, fucked myself silly on a bare wooden floor with someone who chanted Sufi suras. I lost six weeks of my sophomore year because they put me away for trying to jump off the top floor of the Administration Building. Am I scaring you?

Max The corporate gossip says you're Frank Hatchett's backstage floozie.

Diana Frank's a corporation man, body and soul. He has no loves, lusts or allegiances that are not consummately directed towards becoming a CCA board member. So why should he bother with me? I'm not even a stockholder.

Max How about *your* loves, lusts and allegiances?

Diana Is your wife in town?

Max Yes.

Diana We better go to my place.

SCENE NINETEEN
HOWARD ON TV

Howard sits at his desk and addresses the audience, his image large and repeated on the bank of screens. No cameramen and paraphernalia – it's just Howard on set.

Howard Last night I was awakened from a fitful sleep by a shrill, faceless voice from a figure sitting in my rocking chair. I couldn't make it out at first in the dark bedroom. I said, 'I'm sorry, you'll have to talk a little louder.' And the Voice said to me, 'I want you to tell the people the truth, not an easy thing to do, because the people don't want to know the truth.' I said, 'You're kidding. How the hell would I know what the truth is?' But the Voice said to me, 'Don't worry about the truth. I'll put the words in your mouth.' And I said, 'What is this, the burning bush? For God's sake, I'm not Moses.' And the Voice said to me, 'And I'm not God, what's that got to do with it?' And the Voice said 'We're not talking about eternal truth or absolute truth or ultimate truth! We're talking about impermanent, transient, human truth! I don't expect you people to be capable of truth! But goddammit, you're at least capable of self-preservation! That's good enough!'

The lights go out on Howard but his speech continues on the monitors around the auditorium and we find ourselves in Max's office, where Max and Hunter are watching the performance on a TV monitor.

(*On TV.*) 'I want you to go out and tell people to preserve themselves.'

Hunter What do you want me to do?

Max Nothing. Right now I'm just trying to remember the psychiatrist that took care of him when his wife died.

Diana comes in, watches Max.

Howard (*on TV*) And I said to the Voice. 'Why me?' And the Voice said: 'Because you're on television, dummy.'

Diana Beautiful.

Howard (*on monitor*) 'You have forty million Americans listening to you. After tonight's show you could have fifty million.'

Howard himself walks into the room. He watches himself without saying anything.

(*On TV.*) 'For Pete's sake, I don't expect you to walk the land in sackcloth and ashes preaching the Armageddon.

41

You're on teevee, man!' So I thought for a moment. And then I said 'OK.'

Max turns the TV off.

Max I'm taking you off the air, Howard. I'm calling your psychiatrist.

Howard This is not a psychotic episode. It is a cleansing moment of clarity. I am imbued, Max. I am imbued with a special spirit. A shocking eruption of great electrical energy as if suddenly I had been plugged into some great cosmic electromagnetic field. I feel connected to some great unseen force – what, I think, the Hindus call Prana.

Max Howard, I think you are having a breakdown.

Howard I have never felt so orderly in my life. It is a shattering and beautiful sensation. I feel on the verge of some great ultimate truth. You will not take me off air, Max, not now nor any other goddam time.

Max You are losing your mind, Howard. You're becoming a dupe for this stupid organisation. You don't have to do this.

Howard Max, I am impelled to do this. This is my calling. And neither you nor anyone else is going to stand in my goddam way.

Max OK, Howard, but at least come home with me and get a good night's sleep.

SCENE TWENTY
HOWARD AT MAX'S PLACE

We move to Max's house. Thunder. Rain outside. Night. Max's wife Louise is helping Max make up a bed on a sofa.

42

Louise Last night you don't come back at all. Tonight you show up with the raving Jeremiah.

Max I'm sorry, I couldn't leave him. He's mad as a snake.

Howard comes in in his pyjamas, completely calm.

Howard Thank you, Lou, I really don't mean to put you out.

Louise It's OK. You can stay as long as you want, Howard. Nightcap?

Howard I think I need one.

Louise Honey?

Max Sure.

She goes to prepare some drinks.

Listen, Howard, I'm pulling the plug on this whole screwball angry prophet thing. Tomorrow night we're going back to straight news.

Howard You can't do that, Max.

Max You're making a jackass out of me, Howard. You're making a jackass out of yourself. Everyone's just gotten a little overexcited. Let's just go back to what we do.

Howard What we do is lie, Max.

Max I'll find you this drink.

He leaves Howard on his own and joins his wife.

Louise Where were you last night, Max?

Max I told you, I stayed with Howard.

As Max and his wife have their scene, Howard is on his own again. He seems attentive to some unseen force.

Louise Howard called here at three in the morning looking for you.

Max is busted but we concentrate on Howard.

Howard (*addressing the unseen force*) Yes, I am coming. I am coming.

Howard gets up and leaves.

Louise What is going on?

Max Nothing is going on. It's been a very difficult week.

He kisses her, takes the two glasses of whisky out of her hands and goes back to where Howard was sitting.

Howard? Howard?

SCENE TWENTY-ONE
HACKETT'S OFFICE

Hackett What do you mean, you don't know where he is? The son of a bitch is a hit, goddammit, Over two thousand phone calls. Go down to the mailroom. As of this minute, over fourteen thousand telegrams. The response is sensational. Harry, tell him. Harry's phone hasn't stopped ringing. Every goddam affiliate from Albuquerque to Sandusky. The response is sensational. We've got a goddam hit, a goddam hit. Diana, show him the *Times*. We've got an editorial in the holy goddam *New York Times*. That crazy son of a bitch Beale has caught on. So don't tell me you don't know where he is.

Max I don't know where he is. He may be jumping off a roof for all I know. He needs care and treatment. He's manifestly losing his mind and all you graverobbers are concerned about is he's a hit.

Diana But Max, what if he is in fact imbued with some special spirit?

Max My God, *I'm* supposed to be the romantic. You're supposed to be the hard-bitten realist.

Diana All right. Howard Beale obviously fills a void. The audience out there obviously wants a prophet, even a manufactured one, even if he's as mad as Moses. By tomorrow he'll have a 50 share, maybe even a 60. Howard Beale is processed instant God, and right now it looks like he may just go over bigger than Mary Tyler Moore.

Max I'm not putting Howard back on air. We're going back to straight news.

Hackett You don't get to say jack shit, Schumacher, you don't even know where he is.

Diana Anyway, it's not your show any more, Max. It's mine.

Hackett I gave her the show, Schumacher. I'm putting the network news under Programming.

Max Does Ruddy know about this?

Hackett Mr Ruddy has had a mild heart attack and is not taking calls.

Max A heart attack!

Hackett He'll live, most likely. But in his lamented absence, I'm making all network decisions, including one I've been wanting to make a very long time. You're fired. I want you out of this building by the time this show starts. I'll leave word with the security guards to throw you out if you're still here.

Max Well, let's just say fuck you, Hackett. You want me out, you're gonna have to drag me out kicking and screaming. And the whole News Division kicking and screaming with me.

Hackett You think they're going to quit their jobs for you? Not in a recession, buddy.

Max When Ruddy gets back he'll have your ass.

Hackett I got a hit, Schumacher, and Ruddy doesn't count any more. He was hoping I'd fall on my face with this Beale show, but I didn't. It's a big, fat, big-titted hit, and I don't have to waffle around with Ruddy any more. If he wants to take me up before the CCA board let him. And do you think Ruddy's stupid enough to go to the CCA board and say, 'I'm taking our one hit show off the air'? And come October fourteen, I'm going to be standing up there at the annual CCA management review meeting, and I'm going to announce projected earnings for this network for the first time in five years. And believe me, Mr Jensen will be sitting there rocking back and forth in his little chair, and he's gonna say, 'That's very good, Frank, keep it up. So don't have any illusions about who's running this network from now on. You're fired.

Harry Hunter What are we going to do? It's three minutes to.

Hackett Put Snowden on while we track down Beale. (*To Max.*) I want you out of your office before noon. Or I'll have you thrown out.

Max And you're going to go along with this?

Diana Well, Max, I told you I didn't want any network hassle. I told you I'd much rather work the Beale show out just between the two of us.

Max Well, let's just say fuck you too, honey. Howard Beale may be my best friend. I'll go to court, I'll put him in a hospital before I let you exploit him like a carnival freak.

Hackett You get your psychiatrists, and I'll get mine.

Max I'm going to spread this whole reeking business in every paper and on every network, independent, group and affiliated station in this country. I'm going to make a lot of noise about this.

Hackett Great. We need all the press we can get.

Max stalks out.

(*To Diana.*) Something going on between you and Schumacher?

Diana Not any more.

Hackett Where the fuck is Howard Beale?

SCENE TWENTY-TWO
HOWARD RETURNS TO THE NIGHTLY NEWS

The studio team rush to get Snowden ready to go on camera. Diana is watching anxiously as Snowden is miked up in Howard's chair. Hackett is stalking behind Diana.

Hackett This is a fucking disaster. How could you have lost the most famous man on television?

Diana Is Snowden ready?

Director (*through the intercom*) Is Snowden ready?

Floor Manager We are just sorting out the sound.

Harry Hunter Hell of a way to start your first show.

Diana Bang goes my career.

Floor Manager Twenty-five seconds.

Hackett I thought you said you'd find him. / I've put my ass on the line for this stupid schmuck.

Director Quiet in the studio. Give me Camera-A.

Floor Manager Check.

Director Sound?

Floor Manager Not yet.

Director Camera-B.

Floor Manager Check.

Director Sound?

Sound Guy Ready.

Floor Manager Jack is ready. We have sound.
Studio ready. Clear positions.
We have clearance.

In the control room the countdown starts:

Production Assistant Ten . . . nine . . . eight . . . seven . . . six . . . five . . .

Director Continuity.

The Continuity Announcer appears on the monitors telling us:

Continuity Announcer It's time for *Tonight*, with Jack Snowden.

Director Cue music.

Production Assistant Three . . . two . . . one.

The theme music blasts out, the Floor Manager is shouting over the top of this:

Director Titles, credits, camera and action!

Snowden Good evening. It is Thursday, October the second. This is Jack Snowden and this is the news.

Howard arrives in the studio in a raincoat over his pyjamas, soaked to the skin.

Howard Stop!

Snowden is stunned by the intrusion.

I have come to make my witness.

Diana Put him on.

The cameras follow Howard as he takes his seat.

Howard I don't have to tell you things are bad. Everybody knows things are bad. Everybody's out of work or scared of losing their job, the dollar buys a nickel's worth, banks are going bust, shopkeepers keep a gun under the counter, punks are running wild in the streets, and there's nobody anywhere who seems to know what to do and there's no end to it.

We know the air's unfit to breathe and our food is unfit to eat and we sit and watch our teevees while some local newscaster tells us today we had fifteen homicides and sixty-three violent crimes, as if that's the way it's supposed to be. We all know things are bad. Worse than bad. They're crazy. It's like everything's going crazy. So we don't go out any more. We sit in the house and slowly the world we live in gets smaller and all we ask is, please, at least leave us alone in our own living rooms. Let me have my toaster and teevee and my hairdryer and my steel-belted radials and I won't say anything, just leave us alone. Well, I'm not going to leave you alone. I want you to get mad.

He gets up from his desk and walks to the front of the set.

Diana Oh my God, he's good.

49

Howard I don't want you to protest. I don't want you to riot. I don't want you to write to your congressmen. Because I wouldn't know what to tell you to write. I don't know what to do about the depression and the inflation and the defence budget and the Russians and crime in the street. All I know is, first you've got to get mad. You've got to say: 'I'm a human being, goddammit. My life has value.' So I want you to get up right now. I want you to get out of your chairs and go to the window. Right now. I want you to go to the window, open it and stick your head out and yell. I want you to yell, 'I'm mad as hell and I'm not going to take this any more.'

Diana How many stations does this go out to?

Hunter Sixty-seven. I know it goes to Louisville and Atlanta. I think –

Howard Get up from your chairs. Go to the window. Open it. Stick out your head and yell. And keep yelling. First you've got to get mad. When you're mad enough we'll figure out what to do. Stick your head out and yell, 'I'm mad as hell and I'm not going to take it any more.' 'I'm mad as hell and I'm not going to take it any more.' 'I'm mad as hell and I'm not going to take it any more.'

A Technician in the studio shouts out:

Technician I'm mad as hell and I'm not going to take it any more.

Howard That's right. I'm mad as hell and I'm not going to take it any more.

Diana Do we have an outside broadcast?

Director Joe's in Atlanta.

Harry Hunter Show me Atlanta.

They look at the outside broadcast. They are yelling in Atlanta.

Diana Put them on.

On the screens in the studio the outside broadcasts.

Outside Broadcaster They're yelling down here in Atlanta. 'We're mad as hell and we're not going to take it any more.'

Diana They're yelling down in Atlanta, Howard.

Howard That's right. First, you've got to get mad. When you're mad enough, we'll figure out what to do with it.

Diana Get me the OB in Baton Rouge.

Baton Rouge comes up.

They're yelling! They're yelling!

Hackett Holy Jesus Fuck.

Howard I'm mad as hell and I'm not going to take it any more.

Production Assistant I'm mad as hell and I'm not going to take this any more.

Other voices join in from around the studio.

Howard That's it. I've had it with the foreclosures and the oil crisis and the unemployment and the corruption of finance and the inertia of politics and the right to be alive and the right to be angry. I want to hear the little man and woman – I want to hear you now – go to your windows – yell out so they can hear you – yell and don't stop yelling – so the whole world can hear you – above the chaos and degradation the apathy and white noise

Diana They're yelling in Chicago, Howard.

Howard They're yelling in Chicago.

Yell, yell, and then we'll work out what to do about terrorism and the oil crisis. Stick your head out of the window and shout it with me: 'I'm mad as hell and I'm not going to take it any more. I'm mad as hell and I'm not gonna take this any more. I'M MAD AS HELL AND I'M NOT GOING TO TAKE IT ANY MORE.'

The screens show more people joining in the chant.

Diana (*over the address system*) Son of a bitch. We've hit the mother lode.

Act Two

Hackett addressing an audience:

Hackett UBS was running at a cashflow break-even point after taking into account 110 million dollars of negative cashflow from the network. It was clear the fat on the network had to be shaved off.

Perhaps graphs illustrate his talk.

Please note the increase in projected initial programme revenues in the amount of 21 million dollars due to the phenomenal success of *The Howard Beale Show.*
I expect a positive cashflow for the entire complex of forty-five million achievable in this fiscal year, a year, in short, ahead of schedule. But I go beyond that. This network may well be the most significant profit centre of the communications complex –

A close-up of Hackett is projected on the screen behind him.

– and based upon the projected rate of return on invested capital, and if the merger is eventually accomplished, the communications complex may well become the towering and most profitable centre in the entire CCA empire. I await your questions and answers. Mr Jensen.

Jensen's voice:

Jensen (*out of view*) Very good, Frank. Exemplary. Keep it up.

SCENE TWO
DIANA TALKS TO THE TERRORISTS

Diana is alone. On the phone.

Diana This is Diana Christiensen. Director of
Programming at UBS and producer of *The Howard
Beale Show*. I've seen your footage of Detriot and I'd
like to talk to you about an idea I have for a series. I
believe television should tell the whole story and I think
this could get very good ratings. I understand you are
essentially a terrorist organisation but do you have a
lawyer I could talk to?

SCENE THREE
THE NEWS

Warm-up Guy.

Warm-up Guy It's really great to have you all here this
evening. Really great. Did you hear the news this
afternoon? Oh, there was some very interesting news this
afternoon. Amnesty International have come out against
marriage?
  Think about it.
  It was only a matter of time, ladies and gentlemen.
  Let me ask you a question:
  How is everybody feeling tonight?
  Hello?
  Is there anybody out there?
  I asked you: How is everybody feeling tonight?

Perhaps a flashing sign shows the catchphrase.

Voices from the Audience We're mad as hell and we're
not gonna take it any more.

Warm-up Guy I'm sorry. I didn't quite catch that.

Voices from the Audience We're mad as hell and we're not gonna take it any more.

Warm-up Guy That's more like it. And one last time . . .

Voices from the Audience WE'RE MAD AS HELL AND WE'RE NOT GONNA TAKE IT ANY MORE!

Warm-up Guy We've got a really great show for you this evening. Pop Vox and his Street Talkin'. Jim Webbing with 'It's the Damn Truth Department'. So sit back, relax and remember the nightly news is all about YOU! So whenever you see this sign –

'Applause'.

You got to clap like hell.

The audience applaud. Harry Hunter is the producer of the show.

Hunter Thirty seconds.

Production Assistant Thirty seconds.

Floor Manager Thirty seconds and counting.

The 'Applause' sign goes again.

Warm-up Guy That's it. Let them hear ya!

Applause over:

Hunter Can we have Howard, please?

Floor Manager Can we have Howard?

Production Assistant Continuity on air in twenty-three seconds.

Floor Manager Twenty-three seconds and counting.

While final checks are made we hear more voices from the control room.

Director Check Camera-A.

Floor Manager Check.

Nervous tension, people dash round executing the last-minute technical stuff. Harry Hunter leaves for the control room.

Director Camera-B.

Floor Manager Check.

Director Sound.

Floor Manager Check.

Director Howard.

Floor Manager Check.

We see a plethora of ads for soap powder, tacos, hair products, diarrhoea pills as before.

Director Studio ready?

Floor Manager Studio ready.

In the control room the countdown starts:

Production Assistant Ten . . . nine . . . eight . . .

The ads conclude.

Seven . . . six . . . five . . .

Director Continuity.

The 'Applause' sign comes on. We hear applause.
    The Continuity Announcer appears on the monitors telling us:

Continuity Announcer Ladies and Gentlemen. It's six o'clock and it's time for the *Network News Hour* live from New York, with everybody's favourite Prophet of the Airwaves –

Director Cue music.

Production Assistant Three . . . two . . . one.

Continuity Announcer Mr Hhhhoward Beeeeale!

The new theme music blasts out, the Floor Manager is shouting over the top of this:

Director Titles, credits, camera and *Howard*!

Music soars into an imperial crescendo.
A fake stained-glass window.
A dramatic shaft of light picks out Howard looking austere in a black suit and tie.
Tumultuous applause.

Howard Edward George Ruddy died today! Edward George Ruddy was the Chairman of the Board of Union Broadcasting Systems. And he died at eleven o'clock this morning of a heart condition. And woe is us, we're in a lot of trouble. So a rich little man with white hair died, what's that got to do with the price of rice, right? Why is that woe to us? Because you and 62 million other Americans are watching me right now, that's why. Because less than three per cent of you people read books. Because less than fifteen per cent read newspapers. Because the only truth you know is what you get on your television. There is a whole and entire generation right now who never knew anything that didn't come out of this tube. This tube is gospel. This tube is the ultimate revelation. This tube can make or break presidents, popes and prime ministers. This tube is the most awesome goddam force in the whole godless world! And woe is us if it ever falls into the hands of the wrong people. And that's why woe is us that Edward George Ruddy is dead. Because this network is now in the hands of CCA: the Communications Corporation of America. We've got a new chairman of the board called Frank Hackett sitting in Mr Ruddy's office on the twentieth floor. And when the twelfth largest company in the world controls the most awesome goddam propaganda force in the whole godless world, who knows what shit will be peddled for truth. So listen to me. Television is not the truth. Television is a goddam amusement park. Television is a circus, a carnival, a travelling troupe of acrobats, storytellers, dancers, jugglers, sideshow freaks, lion-tamers and football players. If you want to find out about life go to God, go to your guru, go to yourself, because that's the only place to find it – cos you won't find it here. Don't look to us for Truth – because we just tell you what you want to hear. We'll tell you *Kojak* always gets the killer, and no one gets cancer on the *Archie Bunker Show*. And no matter how much trouble the hero is in, he's always gonna win. We'll tell you any old shit you want to hear. None of it is true. Any idiot knows that. But you people sit there – all of you – day after day, night after night, all ages, colours, creeds – and this is all you know. You're beginning to believe this illusion we're spinning. You're beginning to think this is the true reality and it's your own lives that are unreal. That you are the ones who are inadequate. You *feel* what the tube tells you. You *think* like the tube tells you. You *do* what the tube tells you. You dress like the tube, you eat like the tube, you raise your goddam children like you've seen on the tube. This is mindless madness, you maniacs. In God's name, YOU are the real thing. We're illusions. So turn off your sets. Turn it off and leave it off. Go to your switches, pick up your remote controls and strike us down, put an end to this madness, strike a blow for sanity, right now, in the middle of the show, in the middle of this sentence I'm speaking now. Turn off your TVs and set yourselves free, goddammit.

Howard stands like a preacher.

Director And cut to the ad break.

SCENE FOUR
RUDDY'S FUNERAL

On screen, in the rain.

SCENE FIVE
A NEW YORK STREET

It is snowing.

Max Hi.

Diana Hi. How are you doing, Max?

Max I'm fine.

Diana Really?

Max No. Not really.
I try to keep busy. This is my third funeral in two weeks. I have two other friends in hospital who I visit regularly. I've been to a couple of christenings. All my friends seem to be dying or having grandchildren.

Diana You should be a grandfather about now. You have a pregnant daughter out in Seattle, don't you?

Max Any day now. My wife's out there for the occasion. I've thought of calling you many times.

Diana I wish you had. My intimate involvement with a craggy middle-aged man turned out to be just one many-splendoured evening. It was a many-splendoured evening, was it not?

Max Yes, it was.

Diana Are we going to get involved, Max?

Max I need to get involved very much. How about you?

Diana I've reached for the phone so many times, but I was sure you hated me for my part in taking your news show away.

Max I probably did. I don't know any more. All I know is I can't keep you out of my mind.

Diana I'd say what we have here, Max, is a modern-day Greek drama. Two star-crossed lovers. An unhappily married middle-aged man meets desperately lonely career woman. He abandons the devoted wife and children and they fall dementedly in love. Till one of his children is rushed to hospital with a mysterious disease. He goes back to his family, and she is left to throw herself on the railroad tracks. Give me a two-page outline, I might be able to sell it. What are you doing for supper, Max?

SCENE SIX
CANDLELIT SUPPER

Holding hands, looking in one another's eyes.

Diana NBC's offering three-point-two million for a pack of five James Bond pictures but I think I can steal them for three-point-five including a third run.

The *Vigilante* show is sold firm. Ford took a whole thing at, so help me, five fifty-five per episode! In fact, I'm moving the *Vigilante* show to nine and I'd like to stick *The Terror Hour* in at eight because we're having a lot of trouble selling *The Terror Hour*.

They start to make out.

Max *The Terror Hour?*

Diana I've done a deal with those guys from Detroit. We're having some heavy legal problems. Two FBI guys turned up in Hackett's office last week and served us with a subpoena. We're gonna get round that by doing the show in collaboration with the News Division so we can stand on the First Amendment: freedom of the press and the right to protect sources. Walter thinks we can knock out the misprision of felony charge but he says absolutely nix on going to series.

They are stripping each other.

They'll hit us with inducement and conspiracy to commit a crime. I say 'Let the government sue us!' We'll take them to the Supreme Court. We'll be front page for months. The *Washington Post* and the *New York Times* will be doing several editorials a week about us.

Max But these are terrorists.

Diana Like they're not gonna do it anyway.

They make love.

People need to look reality in the eye. We'll have more press than Watergate. Six weeks of federal litigation and *The Terror Hour* can start carrying its own time slot. But what's really bugging me is my daytime programming.

Diana is mechanical and orgasms almost immediately, gets up and starts dressing.

NBC's got a lock on daytime with their lousy game shows but I'd like to bust them. I'm thinking of doing a gay soap opera: *The Dykes.*

She finishes buttoning up her blouse.

What do you think?

SCENE SEVEN
BACK AT 'THE HOWARD BEALE SHOW'

Howard Beale gives an oration on 'The Howard Beale Show'.

Howard All right, listen to me. Listen carefully. This is your goddam life I'm talking about today. In this country when one company takes over another company they simply buy up a controlling share of the stock. But first they have to file notice with the government. That's how CCA – the Communications Corporation of America – bought up the company that owns this network. And now somebody's buying up CCA. They filed their notice this morning. Well, just who the hell is the Western World Funding Corporation? It's a consortium of banks and insurance companies who are not buying CCA for themselves but as agents for someone else. Well, who is this someone else? They won't tell you. They won't tell you, they won't tell the Senate, they won't tell the SEC, the FCC, the Justice Department, they won't tell anybody. Because it is private equity – therefore it's none of your business, they say. I say: The Hell it Ain't. Well, I'll tell you who they're buying the CCA for. They're buying it for the Saudi-Arabian Investment Corporation. They're buying it for the Arabs. We know the Arabs control more than sixteen billion dollars in this country. They own a chunk of Fifth Avenue, twenty downtown pieces of Boston, a part of the port of New Orleans, an industrial park in Salt Lake City. They own big hunks of the Atlanta Hilton, the Arizona Land and Cattle Company, part of a bank in California, the Bank of the Commonwealth in Detroit. They control Aramco, so that puts them into Exxon, Texaco and Mobil Oil. They're all over New Jersey, Louisville, St Louis, Missouri. And the majority share of the national debt. And that's just what we know about. There's a hell of a lot more we don't know about because all those Arab petrodollars are washed through Switzerland and Canada and the biggest banks in the country. For example, what we don't know about is this CCA deal and all the other CCA deals. Right now the Arabs have screwed us out of enough American dollars to come back and with our own money buy General Motors, IBM, ITT, AT&T, DuPont, US Steel and twenty other top American companies. Hell, they already own half of England. A handful of agas, shahs and emirs who despise this country and everything it stands for – democracy, freedom, the right for me to get up on television and tell you about it – a couple of dozen mediaeval fanatics are going to own where you work, where you live, what you read, what you see, your cars, your bowling alleys, your mortgages, your schools, your churches, your libraries, your kids, your whole life – and there's not a single law on the books to stop them. Because everything is for sale. It's a global market. The rich are steadily getting richer and they have bought up *you*. And there's only one thing that can stop them. *You.* Now listen to me, goddammit! I want you to get up right now. I want you to get out of your chairs and go to the phone. Right now. I want you to go to your phone or get in your car and drive into the Western Union office in town. I want everybody to get up right now and send a telegram to the White House. By midnight I want a million telegrams in the White House. I want them wading knee-deep in telegrams at the White House saying, 'I'm mad as hell and I'm not going to take this any more.' I want this CCA deal stopped right now.

Lights out on Howard, but the speech continues on a bank of monitors in the control room.

SCENE EIGHT
HACKETT WATCHES BEALE'S DISASTER

We are in Hackett's office and he is watching it on playback with Diana, Chaney and a technical guy.

Hackett Oh God. Oh God.

Howard (*on the monitor*) I want them wading knee-deep in telegrams at the White house saying, 'I'm mad as hell and I'm not going to take this any more.' I want this CCA deal stopped right now.

Hackett freezes the playback.

Diana Is this true, Frank?

Hackett CCA has two billion in loans with the Saudis, and they hold every pledge we've got. We need that Saudi money bad. Disaster. This show is a disaster, an unmitigated disaster, the death knell. I'm ruined, I'm dead, I'm finished.

Chaney Maybe we're overstating Beale's clout with the public.

Hackett An hour ago, Clarence McElheny called me from Washington. It was ten o'clock and our people in the White House report they are already knee deep in telegrams. By tomorrow morning they'll've suffocated.

Chaney Can they stop the deal?

Hackett They can hold it up. The SEC can hold this deal up for twenty years if they want to. I'm finished. Any second that phone's gonna ring and Clarence McElheny's going to tell me Mr Jensen wants me in his office tomorrow morning so he can personally chop my head off. Four hours ago I was the sun god, the hand-picked boy, the heir apparent. Now I'm a man without a corporation. I want him off the air.

Diana We can't just pull the number one show on television out of pique?

Hackett Two billion dollars isn't pique. That's the wrath of fucking God!

64

Diana Every other network will grab him the minute he walks out the door. He'll be back on the air for ABC tomorrow. And we'll lose twenty points in audience share.

Hackett I am going to kill Howard Beale. I'm going to impale the son of a bitch with a sharp stick through the heart.

Chaney Calm down, Frank.

Hackett I'll take out a contract on him. I'll hire professional killers. I'll do it myself. I'll strangle him with a sash cord.

Diana Jensen is a big man. He won't overreact. I don't think he's gonna fire anybody.

The phone rings.

Hackett Hackett. Yes. Mr Jensen . . . Yes, of course, of course . . . Of course. I'll be there.

He puts the phone down.

Mr Jensen wants to see Howard Beale in person. At ten o'clock tomorrow morning.

SCENE NINE
OUTSIDE JENSEN'S OFFICE

Hackett and Howard Beale wait outside Jensen's office.

Hackett You shit. You get down on your fucking knees, Beale, and you plead for fucking mercy.

Howard You don't understand, do you? I can't be bought. I have the power of television with me. And instead of it being used to buy and sell people, finally I am using it to set people free. Jensen doesn't scare me. None of you scare me because this isn't a corporate game any more. The final revelation is at hand. And I come to bear witness to the light.

A Secretary comes out.

Secretary Mr Jensen will see you now.

SCENE TEN
VALHALLA

Jensen's room – more like a cathedral than an office. Howard comes in. Footsteps echo. He can't see Jensen in the gloaming. Anyway, Jensen has his back to us.

Jensen (*unseen, politely*) Sit down, Mr Beale.

Then he switches on the lights, a spotlight on Jensen in his seat. Jensen decorously clears his throat then stands up.

(*With the wrath of God.*) You have meddled with the primal forces of nature, Mr Beale, and I won't have it. Is that clear? You think you have merely stopped a business deal – that is not the case. The Arabs have taken billions of dollars out of this country and now they must put it back. It is ebb and flow, tidal gravity, it is ecological balance. You are an old man who thinks in terms of nations and peoples. There are no nations. There are no peoples. There are no Russians. There are no Arabs. There are no Third Worlds. There is no West. There is only one holistic system of systems, one vast immanent, interwoven, interacting, multi-variate, multinational dominion of dollars. Petrodollars, electro-dollars, multi-dollars, Reichsmarks, roubles, pounds and shekels. It is the international system of currency that determines the totality of life upon this planet. That is the natural order of things today. That is the atomic, sub-atomic and galactic structure of things. And you have meddled with the primal forces of nature and you will atone. Am I getting through to you, Mr Beale? You get up on your little twenty-one inch screen, Mr Beale, and howl about America and democracy. There is no America. There is no democracy. There is only IBM and AT&T and Ford and General Electric, Union Carbide, Exxon. Those are the nations of the world today, but they are not entities like the nation state – they don't actually exist. Where is Coca-Cola? It is a notion. What exists is the primordial movement of capital. We are the flux of commerce, Mr Beale. There is no politics, ideology, just the endless, inexorable movement of money. What do you think the Russians or the Chinese talk about in their councils of state? Karl Marx? They pull out their linear programming charts, statistical decision theories, minimax solutions, and compute the price–cost probabilities of their transactions and investments just like we do. We no longer live in a world of nations and ideologies, Mr Beale. The world is a college of corporations, inexorably determined by the immutable by-laws of business. The world is a business, Mr Beale. It has been that way since man crawled out of the slime and our children, Mr Beale, will live to see that perfect world without war or famine, oppression or brutality – one vast and ecumenical holding company, for whom all men will work to serve a common profit, in which all men will hold a share of stock, all necessities provided, all anxieties tranquillised, all boredom amused.

Howard is in awe.

And I have chosen you to preach this evangel.

Pause.

Howard Why me?

Jensen Because you're on television, dummy. Sixty million people watch you every night of the week.

SCENE ELEVEN
MAX CONFRONTS HIS INFIDELITY

Max and Louise.

Louise How long has this been going on?

Max A month. I thought at first it might be a transient thing and blow over in a week. I still hope to God it's just a menopausal infatuation. But it is an infatuation, Louise. There's no sense my saying I won't see her again, because I will. Do you want me to clear out, go to a hotel?

Louise Do you love her?

Max I don't know how I feel, I'm grateful I still feel anything. I know I'm obsessed with her.

Louise Then say it! Don't keep telling me you're obsessed, you're infatuated – say you're in love with her.

Max I'm in love with her.

Louise Then get out, go to a hotel, go anywhere you want, go live with her, but don't come back. Because after twenty-five years of building a home and raising a family and all the senseless pain we've inflicted on each other I'll be damned if I'll just stand here and let you tell me you love someone else. Because this isn't some convention weekend with your secretary, is it? Or some broad you picked up after three belts of booze. This is your great winter romance, isn't it? Your last roar of passion before you sink into your emeritus years. Is that what's left for me? Is that my share? She gets the great winter passion and I get the dotage? Am I supposed to sit at home knitting and purling till you slink back like a penitent drunk? I'm your wife, damn it. If you can't work up a winter passion for me then the least I require is respect and allegiance. I'm hurt. Don't you understand that? I hurt badly.

Silence.

Say something, for God's sake.

Max I've got nothing to say.

Louise I won't give you up easily, Max. Perhaps it is better if you do move out. Does she love you, Max?

Max I'm not sure she's capable of any real feelings. She's the television generation. She learned life from Bugs Bunny. The only reality she knows is what comes over her teevee set. She has devised a variety of scenarios for us all to play as if it were a Movie of the Week. And my God, look at us, Louise. Here we are going through the obligatory middle of Act Two, scorned-wife-throws-peccant-husband-out scene. But don't worry I'll come back home in the end. All her plot outlines have me leaving her and returning to you, because the audience won't buy a rejection of the happy American family. She does have one script in which I kill myself, an adapted-for-television version of *Anna Karenina* in which she's Count Vronsky and I'm Anna.

Louise You're in for some dreadful grief, Max.

Max I know.

SCENE TWELVE
HOWARD PREACHES THE EVANGEL

Howard Last night I got up here and asked you people to stand up and fight for your heritage and you did. The Arab takeover of CCA has been stopped. A radiant, nostalgic eruption of people power. But we know this isn't how things can be run. Because, in the bottom of all

69

our terrified souls, we know that democracy is a dying giant, a decaying political concept. I don't mean the United States is finished as a world power. The United States is the richest country in the world. What we all know is finished is the idea that any country can be dedicated to the freedom and flourishing of every individual in it. You see, we're no longer a nation of individuals. This is a nation of two-hundred-odd million, transistorised, deodorised, dehumanised beings – mass produced, regulated, programmed to produce and consume other mass-produced products. Well, the time has come to ask: is this such a bad thing? Our bellies are full, our needs are met. Maybe it's time to wake up and realise this is evolution. That what matters is not any single one of us. *We* are not 'the meaning'. Human existence is an *utterly futile and purposeless thing*. Grasp that, the whole damn universe becomes orderly and comprehensible: You have no power, democracy has no power, politicians have no power, nobody really has power. But it works. And how it works is accepting that we are not the emperors of ourselves, we are bees in the hive, it's not our individuality which makes us rich, but our communality. We must ask how we can advance the *whole* rather than ourselves, each one of us just a tiny node in the grand, glorious network.

SCENE THIRTEEEN
RATINGS START TO FALL

Diana The *Beale Show* Q-score is down to thirty-three. With the biggest drop-off in the eighteen to thirty-four categories. That's already a forty 45-million-dollar loss in annual revenues. The affiliates are refusing to follow him. They're pleading with me to take him off the air. They're refusing to follow his goddam show. The man's a plague. He's smallpox. Can't we lay him off? Put him on vacation? If we don't do something, Mr Jensen is gonna kick our sorry asses.

Hackett On the contrary. Mr Jensen is unhappy at the idea of taking Beale off the air. Mr Jensen thinks Howard Beale is bringing a very important message to the American people, so he wants Howard Beale on the air. And he wants him kept on. Where does that put us, Diana?

Diana That puts us in the shithouse, that's where that puts us.

SCENE FOURTEEN
THINGS GO FROM BAD TO WORSE

Howard on a TV screen in Diana's home, the sound turned off as Diana is on the phone.

Diana You're his goddam agent, Lew, I'm counting on you to talk some sense into the lunatic! Nobody wants to hear about the dying of democracy and dehumanisation. We dipped under a 40 share last night. He has to stop. It's killing us. Another couple of weeks and the sponsors will be pulling out all together.

During the call Max has come in. He looks dejected.

This is breach of contract, Lew! You better get him off this corporate kick or so help me I'll pull him off the air . . . I already told him, Lew. I've been telling him every day for a week. I'm sick of telling him. Now you tell him.

She finally slams the phone down.

You know you could help me out with Howard if you wanted to. He listens to you. And I really don't see why you don't talk to him. I thought he was your best friend, for chrissake.

Max Well, I'm just tired by all this hysteria about Howard Beale. And I'm tired of finding you on the goddam phone every time I turn around. I'm tired of being an accessory in your life. After six months of living with you, I'm turning into one of your scripts. But this isn't a script, Diana. There's some real actual life going on here. I went to visit my wife today.

Diana Oh! Really?!

Max Because she's in a state of depression –

Diana Every time you see someone in your family you come back in one of these morbid middle-aged moods

Max She's so depressed my daughter flew in from Seattle to be with her.

Diana And you feel real lousy about that.

Max Yes, I feel lousy about that. I feel lousy about the pain I've caused my wife and kids. I feel guilty and conscience-stricken and all those things you think sentimental but which my generation called simple human decency. And I miss my home because I'm beginning to get scared shitless. It's all suddenly closer to the end than to the beginning, and death is suddenly a perceptible thing to me. You've got a man going through primal doubts, Diana, and you've got to cope with it. Because I'm not some guy discussing male menopause on the Barbara Walters show. I'm the man you presumably love. I'm part of your life. I live here. I'm real. You can't switch to another station.

Diana Well, what exactly is it you want me to do?

Max I just want you to love me. I just want you to love me, primal doubts and all. We're born in terror and we live in terror. Life can be endured only as an act of faith and the only act of faith any of us are capable of is love.

You understand that, don't you?

Diana I don't know how to do that.

The phone rings. They stare at one another. Finally she picks it up.

Yes.

Max You are a wasteland, Diana.

SCENE FIFTEEN
DIANA GOES TO VALHALLA

Jensen's office. Diana and Jensen.

Diana Mr Jensen, sir. As a network we are above taking any ideological positions. News and opinion has to be governed by the same editorial strictures as any other department. But the bottom line is that Beale is dropping like a stone. I have no editorial beef, here, Mr Jensen. I am neutral on all ideological issues – but the ratings have plummeted. This week *The Howard Beale Show* is likely to be the least watched show on the entire evening schedule.

Jensen You don't like Beale's ideas?

Diana I am a television executive. With great respect, Mr Jensen, I couldn't give a flying fuck about ideas. The bottom line is if we don't take Beale off the air he is going to cost us five hundred thousand a week. There is nothing intrinsically wrong with *The Howard Beale Show*. Television is a volatile industry in which success and failure are determined week by week. We have to deal with Beale for the future of the channel.

Jensen May I politely suggest, Ms Christiensen, that volatility in business is often a reflection of poor management. Personally I do not care if Howard Beale is the number one show on television or the fiftieth. I can only imagine your obsession with ratings is due to some very antiquated thinking. The point of a network, Ms Christiensen, is that no one position need take the load – the point of a network is that functionality is spread throughout a system. What kind of television outfit are you running if you can't carry a single goddam programme? Television isn't the 'future' of anything, television is the past. You seem still under some nineteen-sixties delusion that the medium is the message. It is 'ideas' that are important, multivalent, cross-platform: good old-fashioned, immaterial ideas which exist with or without television, Ms Christiensen. Television isn't the message. Television is the hardware – and like any hardware it is prone to obsolescence. The Corporation diversified a long time ago. I've nothing against television, in fact I rather like television and I especially admire Mr Beale.

Diana But it doesn't make any good business sense.

Jensen That's not my problem, Ms Christiensen.

SCENE SIXTEEN
MAX FINALLY GIVES UP ON HOWARD

New York City Bar. Max and Howard in the same state as Act One.

Howard It sounds like a hell of car crash.

Max I am living in a little room on 54th Street. I spend most days writing my memoirs like every other sad sack that got fired in the last decade. Neither of my daughters will speak to me. I miss Louise. I miss you, Howard. What are you doing?

Howard I'm on television, dummy.

Max They're turning off in droves. Surely you don't believe this corporate 'shit' is the truth?

Howard It's as good a truth as any. What good did the angry man stuff do us, Max? Did you see revolution in the streets? I have a wage, I have a purpose. You really want me to give it up after everything? All we wanted was to do our jobs.

Max But Jesus Christ, Howard, surely there has to be some human dignity?

Howard You think we were dignified – lining our pockets like everyone else? Yeah, it felt good being on the crest of a wave – the great new age of television – don't be fooled, we were like every other schmuck and now it's over, gone the way of the pigeon post. Do you really think we were immune and immaculate because we were on TV?

Max You are despicable, Howard. I'm not talking about TV. You're a dupe. It doesn't work. You'll get spat out like the rest of us. So long, Howard, it's been a hell of a ride.

Howard Wait, Max. You don't understand. Max.

Max is gone.

SCENE SEVENTEEN
THE FINAL SOLUTION

Hackett's office. Diana, Hackett, Chaney:

Hackett So we're fucked.

Diana Unequivocably. He wants Howard Beale on the air. And he wants him kept on.

Hackett And you would describe Mr Jensen's position on Beale as inflexible?

Diana Intractable and adamantine.

Chaney This ridiculous whim is gonna take out the whole department.

Hackett This ridiculous whim is gonna take out the entire network. What the hell are we gonna do about it? Kill the son of a bitch?

Diana and Hackett look at one another.

SCENE EIGHTEEN
'THE HOWARD BEALE SHOW'
COMES TO AN END

The studio.

Production Assistant One minute to go.

Floor Manager One minute to go.

Director Can we have Howard, please?

Floor Manager Can we have Howard?

Production Assistant Continuity on air in fifty-five seconds.

Floor Manager Fifty-five seconds and counting. Howard. Where the hell is Howard?

Howard is brought on, followed by his make-up and costume people.

Director Give me Camera-A. Do we have sound?

Floor Manager Check.

Production Assistant Thirty seconds.

Director Camera-B.

Floor Manager Check.

Director Sound.

Floor Manager Check.

Director Howard.

Floor Manager Check.

Director Studio ready?

Floor Manager Studio ready.

Production Assistant Ten . . . nine . . . eight . . . seven . . . six . . . five . . .

Director Continuity.

Continuity Announcer It's time for *Tonight*, with Howard Beale.

Director Cue music.

Production Assistant Three . . . two . . . one.

Director Titles, credits, camera, and *Howard*!

Howard comes out to receive his applause.

Howard All right, all right. Enough of this charade. I have something serious to say to you. I've had enough.

Diana Oh God. The son of a bitch is gonna resign.

Hackett Jesus Christ.

Howard And so Howard Beale became the only TV personality who died because of bad ratings. But here is the truth – the 'absolute truth', paradoxical as it might appear. The thing we must be most afraid of is the destructive power of absolute beliefs – that we can know anything conclusively, absolutely – whether we are compelled to it by anger, fear, righteousness, injustice, indignation; as soon as we have ossified that truth, as soon as we start believing in that absolute – we stop believing in human beings, as mad and tragic as they are. The only total commitment any of us can have is to other people – in all their complexity, in their otherness, their intractable reality . . . This is truly what I believe: it is not ideas that matter, it is human beings. This is Howard Beale signing off for the very last time.

A man in a suit climbs onstage from the audience and shoots Howard calmly in the head. He fires around the studio as he shouts:

Terrorist We reject all media. All representation. All spectacle and distortion.

He shoots himself.